David Thomas

Fossil Fuel

Blue Horse Press

Blue Horse Press
P.O. Box 7000 - 760
Redondo Beach, California 90277
2015

First published by Montana Writers Cooperative

Copyright © 1977, 2015 by David Thomas
Reprinted by permission of the author

Preface copyright © 2015 David E. Thomas

Cover illustration by Frank Dugan

Title illustration by
Jay Rummel
Founder of the Montana School
Of Fantastic Country Western
Realism

Photo by Bob Cushman

to all "Montana Hoochies"
everywhere
and the bartenders who must
put up with 'em

PREFACE
BLUE HORSE PRESS EDITION
FOSSIL FUEL

You never know what might happen. Almost twenty years ago returning from a reading with Writer's Voice in Billings, Montana, Mark Gibbons and I stopped in Livingston and I left a couple copies of my book *Buck's Last Wreck* in a small bookstore there, I thought no more about it until recently Barbara Theroux at Fact'n Fiction Bookstore here in Missoula asked me to sign a copy of my book *The Hellgate Wind* and then a couple weeks later a copy of my latest book to date *Waterworks Hill* and on that occasion asked about the availability of my first book *Fossil Fuel*. I replied that I had none available but that if someone wanted to finance a press run I supposed that it could become so. I then learned that the person who'd been buying my books and having me sign them was Jeffrey Alfier and that he'd come across *Buck's Last Wreck* in that Livingston bookstore and that after reading it in his Billings hotel room he became interested in seeing more of my work and that further he might be interested in reprinting *Fossil Fuel* through his Blue Horse Press. I got in touch and here we are with my first book again available in print warts and all.

So I want to thank Jeff Alfier for his efforts here and also give a nod of acknowledgement to Peter Koch for his design of the original edition and to my old pal Frank Dugan for the cover art. I offer posthumous acknowledgement to Jay Rummel for the title page illustration and to Bob Cushman for the back cover photo. I would also like to acknowledge the members of "The Montana Writer's Cooperative" which supported the original publication of *Fossil Fuel*; Jane Bailey, Michael Fiedler, Peter Koch, Shelley Hoyt-Koch, Patrick Todd and myself. The original typesetting was done by Borrowed Times Graphics (later

Arrow Graphics) and the printing done by a small press near Saint Ignatius on the Flathead Reservation.

I should also mention that several of the poems in *Fossil Fuel* were first published in *Montana Gothic* magazine edited by Peter Koch and that the poem "Santos Going Fishing" appears in my book *Buck's Last Wreck* and the poems "Milk River Birthday", "The End of Autumn" and "The National Museum of Anthropology of Mexico" also appear in my book *The Hellgate Wind.* My thanks to everyone who helped me produce those books and for the enormous amount of help I've received over the years.

I would like to further mention that while recently attending my 50th high school class reunion one of my classmates remarked to me that in searching the internet for some clue as to my existence she noticed that there was a vast number of people named either "David Thomas" or "David E. Thomas" who had published poetry in some form so since this slim volume first appeared under the appellation "David Thomas" and all subsequent books under "David E. Thomas" I am retaining "David Thomas" as the appellation for *Fossil Fuel* and would like to state that for copyright purposes in this instance "David Thomas" and "David E. Thomas" are one and the same person should anyone ever become confused on that point.

David E. Thomas
October 1, 2015

NOCTURNAL HISTORY MISSOULA YARDS

hi speed freeway buzz high rapping
wind early
autumn morning
stars ring a gentle chill
I know my way home past wreckt
freight cars
on lonely sidetrack
great yardlights blare
out silence
the idle throb of waiting
diesel thuds
the air as hoofs of bison
antelope deer
and elk pound
the deep prairies of other times
driving grasses and berries
to fossilization
that today howls and whines
a dying purple
a gold goodbye.

23 sept 74
missoula

NOTES ON A GANDY STORY

a dumb silence — mute birds call imaginary notes — the last feeling passd away — he pickt up his hammer bent to the spike drove it down remembered his back stood up — a hundred years — more — this same dull process — the twin rails stretched into a curve blended with a cliff around the river — a line of men — spread out — doing by hand what machines were meant to do, merely to put in time — to be there for the eight hours — to earn the pay — snow on the higher peaks — spring or autumn? The heat of summer either dread premonition or still quivering memory of monotonous agony. time bends. time melts. a hundred years, more — how long had he been here? whose body was this that bent and groand? he mirrored the questions — rocks skippt the river — the slow mindless flow hiding fish in murky holes — "I love her" he thinks "she's some feeling I have pulls me in this river drops me in these holes pulls me out like a sucker or carp throws me back still swimming always swimming these same dull strokes" — another spike nailed steel rail to wooden tie — the sharp sounds of his own work dissolve his thoughts — his arms back legs serve his eyes — lost in a process — a sensation reacting to ancient fears survive —

conquer — build — never falter (death) the sun glares along the rails dust clouds briefly as his booted feet inch from tie to tie — warm thoughts of breasts lips cunts comfort him — he scratches himself feels a brief hardness sighs aims the hammer again — long handled, wide slender head a shadow across his body to top the spike with a ringing blow — youthful athletic failures stream out in vapors of diluted anguish — hits the spike again — fantasy touchdowns unmade tackles fear of contact fear of involvement resolved in quick hard moments of spikes piercing wood — sweat runs into his eyes clouds his vision he rubs them clear with a grimy hand — red rimmed ache how long 'till quittin' time? 'till crowded hours of noisy bars frantic beers jukeboxes and loose women? how long? he steps off the tracks pees a pale yellow stream into nearby wildrose bushes "HOT RAIL!" the yell goes the line — everybody steps back a freight's coming thru — a dull diesel throb roaring up a thunder of big engines and train of cars rolling screech wheeld past a knot of tired men — the caboose drags the noise away in untold haste — a whiff of pine needles. the clear sky broken by fluffs of cloud passing. "pick up the tools let's go home" — the dumb silence falls into relieved conversation — free to go home — free to chase their dreams — they walk down the tracks — lost in the world each stranger to the other going separate ways only to meet in crowded saloons in clean clothes to drink away time waste away time — knowing each other's life is his own and knowing too, an awful solitude — a dumb silence — and hopes no paycheck will bring.

12 nov 74

AFTERWORK MEDITATION

    hi – speed freight cars
            bounce
              across
          rail joint
        one bolt's loose
            jiggles

        laid two ribbons today
           held up a freight
                so long they
            rerouted him
                    to Whitefish

    big deal
        tomorrow's Friday

gather up laundry.

19 june 74
hope, idaho

GREENOUGH PARK GOOF

   a dammd up pool
      dead leaves crisp yellow
         above mossy rocks
   Rattlesnake Creek
   steel bosses on the street
       don't even smile
           or wave
   a burst of pretty girls
      thru afternoon bars
   last night's hugs warm me
   like wet rotting wood
   steel gang dirt slowly
         washes away.

(respect to John Stromnes
who showed me how this poem
should go.)

22 oct 75
missoula

THE END OF AUTUMN

    the dance of night clouds
            breaks open
              starlight
  flanks of Mount Jumbo
          Mount Sentinel
     shiver the coming
        of first snow
  hard moments of anger boil
     beneath my reason
       my soul feels
       long fingers
  itching for Mexican beaches
      the silver light
        of tropical night
  stirs my memory – I hear
      the freights
  clack a metallic brake
  soon they'll ease out
         East or West
    a slow rumble
    a steady roar
  this waiting watching
     the snow inch down

    from high peaks
        to this lowest
          valley of all
    my nose smells deep jungles
            and unknown eyes
          wink in my sleep

13 nov 74
missoula

SANTOS GOING FISHING

a portrait without paints
      visions behind eyes
   the open sea – sharp empty air
    warm this far south
     even now snow and cold
    have captured the mountains
of home, his face is round
          and quick
   mouth full of rapid Spanish
      skin brown
     with ancestry and sun
      eyes flick across
        waves
    catching sign of fish
        perchd on gunnel
   he hauls up lobster trap
   bare feet like pelican claws
      a stocky walk
        over rock and sand
   he cooks with ferocity
        knows the power
         of his spices
   his "machina" runs on constant

care – parts
are hard to find
his sierra line comes in fighting
will his boat be full?
"Aiyee!!" he cries
shakes his head
a greenhorn falls in his boat
he pours "l' alcohol" in his "cafe"
waits for supper by oil light
a cigarette
dangles – straw hat and sandals
the portrait
is never finished
of Santos going fishing

14 dec 73
chacala, nay, mexico

AT THE RUINAS

the insect world sneaks out
        all hours
          in varied formations
     seeking blood
       sucking blood
          traveling ancient
lines on fresh bodies of meat.

    deep rains – coastal clouds
a dark region encountered
      by seers of light
great Mayan telepathic station
       crossroads
     of many worlds
 the human element – carved in stone
    hidden in darkness
     ancient pictures
  welts on the skin of stone
     old priests
       educate their
      victims
     slab of stone
staind red with centuries
       sacrificial rain

    the grayness – stark
        old bone
   uncovered by dogs with loudspeakers
it was time – unknown symbols draw
       pictures in "turistas" dreams
"El Sol" back bent like Atlas
    in Greece
the Mediterranean
  the Caribbean
great crescents of saltwater
drawing light/heat inland
   stone towers
  toppt with strange antenna
huge crypts – the final waiting
      room
 the last trip – extraterrestrial
 the other side of space – what goes on
    inside
      those twinkles?
at the bottom of the pyramid
  a sarcophagus
    a great stone slab
 carved in the light
    of unknown history
reveald again
    on the edge

      of florida
              breast shaped
             cone – nipple
    to the vast unknown
        flamed from Earth
   a message in mass
   an energy splurt
grown organically the prize of games
            playd by scholars
              on the dreams
  of dreamers who've
       restd
     their case
    in carvings
      on stone.

22 dec 73
palenque, chis, mexico

MEXICO CITY THE WORLD MAP

if I start without
        within what
      am I?
  where do I end up
      if the bus doesn't stop?
is there a border?
        does it mean language
      or the way a flower
        has petals
      a center
        of pollen
      a seed center
    a mouth sucking bee
      legs
    dropping out dry
silence autumn wind
    drives hither and yon
        husks covered with
snow guard the first breath
  a new being
melt soaks it into
      ground
the gnawing ache
        roots growing out
    seeking soil and moisture
    soothing the pain with green

                    shoots
              cracking the surface
           the first leaf meets light
         spreads and is joined
                by more
                   all spreading
              a great shade
                for ants
                    on their trails
              for squirrels hiding nuts
                birds to rest
                man to be cool

  if I start within
              without what
                    am I?
        a city roars in the night
            blows neon
            in a thousand
                    directions
    spews people in hordes
                 streaming
         thru mazes upon mazes
         riding subways beneath buses
                to bedrooms of solitude
            waiting
                waiting
                    waiting

      for some unknown
        but promised end
    seeds grow in windowsill
           pots
wilt in smogs of insanity
         maskd as desire
within what to do I wait
       for who?
I see faces hidden in rock
       crack before
     seed pressures
    and bear leaves
to a sun light that no longer
         hears
    the snarling groan
      of internal
        combustion
faces that smile in fissures
      gargle in their depths
     a molten
   phlegm that burns
            and burns
a clear flowing heat
    that carves and
         carves

11 jan 74

THE NATIONAL MUSEUM OF ANTHROPOLOGY, MEXICO

in rooms of glass (high walls)
        skulls ribs vertebrae
        leg bones arm bones
           finger bones
       gut feelings humming
   jungles and barren plateaus
       pyramids tower
in bone-like dignity, clusterd
       in dead cities
          they grow a flesh
          of ferns and vines
     their secrets mumble
         like deaf dogs
          begging tourist eyes
         for a bone
bones, bones, pots and bones –
    how many bones
      can turn
      your mind?
men with shiny buttons and shoes
      walk around all day
    guns on their hips protecting
      the dead
   All these things
     these big stone faces

        fading in agony
    strange heads like deformd
        children carved out of time
who did this?
      outside these rooms
    a roar of fossil fuel
and people with skin
      the color of volcanos
      and eyes that see thru dreams
    they are shining
    my boots and wearing sandals.

17 dec 74 (22 may 75)
mex city (missoula)

CULTURAL CONTRASTS IN NATIONAL MUSEUM OF COSTA RICA

   jaguar god of the jungle prowls
       with ears of corn heapt
           on his back
he snarls thru stone a terrible visage
            his breath
     curls like incense
      in dark rooms beneath a pyramid
              of huge steps
    corn is ground into flesh
         patiently a stone rolls
           to and fro
  corn is planted by movements of the sun
      chartd against revelations
          at midnight
  and secrets whispered at high tide
jaguar watches over pointed sticks with dark eyes
    flashing death
      does he hear the clanking
        of armor the plodding of horses?
does he smell the gunpowder that is seeking him?
      quickly they bury his monuments
        the jungle grows over
           his footprints
the king of spain flies from a wooden pole

        the jungle and mountaintops
    are divided into geography and occupied
by soldiers whose names are remembered in school
       a rate of exchange establishd
             and currency mintd
     cities grow and receive ambassadors
           now and then jaguar eats
            a horse
   causes a minor upheaval the regime
               changes
and life goes on poked in the earth
         with pointd sticks
  a stone face of bared fangs hidden
         in an air-conditioned room
    watches with empty eyes.

4 jan 76
san jose c.r.

QUITO

tiny insects build an empire
        of welts
– succulent turista flesh!
warm afternoon draws flies
        huge Saturday
market they buzz entrails
  and jawbones of cattle
    inspect pig snouts
        dive into limonada
dusty Indian women offer potatoes
              onions
  ground maize and other flours
    tumult of flesh
        running like a stream
          over rocks
  fedoras and rubber boots
      young boys dart over garbage
            piles
  the city shimmers white
    in clear air
inside a cathedral vast geometries
    of gold leaf assail humble minds
protecting plaster saints from legless beggars
        and pregnant women
  in volcano shadows an old drunk
    stretches out on a sidewalk

                whole beat families
            seek these shadows
above the sprawling city
      perched on a crescent moon
          riding serpentine clouds
      atop the globe
a headless armless statue stands
       its face in a wooden crate
           below - its hand crated too
a hollow steel hand
         I've seen on countless
              plaster Christs offering
                    peace to the world
far below the market teems
        bits of color
antlike with distance up close
            a human face
does the Inca still watch over this plateau?
        ancient eyes
        knowing past
              countless rulers
        a hard-on wind
          blue sky vagina
        dark clouds
        rain drops - - -

17 jan 76
quito equador

RIGHT AT HOME IN CUENCA

sad streets weary with people
   paved with hard-eyed sympathy
      quarried from a hot moment
this burden of old rags breathes shit
      and envies dogs
a haughty student flashes red stars
     from eyeballs
        of socialist fancy
this burden of old rags teems lice
      and begs volcanoes to erupt
   sad streets paved with cripples
     a squashd avocado
    slick seed in the gutter
     growing grooves
   of empty cigarette wrappers
    old eyes blank
     with wrinkles
   stories of pain etcht
       in outstretched palms
it is too bad whole streets of people
   are born without newspapers
     taking note
that hordes live and die anonymous
     like mosquitos in a snap frost
what is this human crying for alms?

        moaning chant of old women
        besieging cafes with their sagging
                flesh
        a rattling of small coins starts a riot
                of hungry eyes
        insulation of money belts
        sensitive fat of good leather
        on sad pavements made dangerous
                by a barricade of eyes
inarticulate termites gnaw
    huge rolls of newsprint to dust
cities of the famished are built
    from discarded corn flakes
a fierce telepathy of howling drums
            paints a slogan on starving walls
            everyone hears it pulls
in their heart a beat of pure space avenging
            delusions of skyscrapers
                and freeways
there is a fast council of beggars and buses
        to decide a treaty
            with the wind
        dark clouds move to adjourn
            but no vote is taken
there is a damp hand on my sleeve
        and a wide eyed kid
                wants to see a movie

READING AIMEE CESAIRE IN QUITO

far from my home in hi-line snow
    I hear a black man's song
sung like blood wrenchd from the sun
      it runs thru my ears
   like molten gold and burns
         in my eyes
            a fresh vision
of salt water and pelicans
        diving in quick breezes
a bus horn blows me back to cold prairies
   I huddle under stiff buffalo robe
         and count my sins
   the breath of Coyote is on my back
       that I am a nephew
            of Trickster
   sticks in my craw the concrete
        of Libby Dam hardens
to my feet as I cross the equator
      searching for an end
to this owl-hooting that weaves
        my dreams from milk river
mud to these misty Andino heights
        I am lost and a compass
of bone rattling sorrows does not speak
        to the four winds like a fire

of rocks I once knew deep song
        of the Bitterroots old wrinkle face
          grandmother of sweat lodges
              tempting me to die
              tempting me to live
I came down from her mountain
        got drunk under a bridge
and ran with a fast woman
        to the site of fool's gold
mined in the shadow of a dam
      I followd a rerouted river
      to the end of fame
woke up smelling of sagebrush
        and coyote piss
  under a sky of nameless stars
        a black man sings his song
        in this city below the equator
        in a silence of taxis and buses
I listen to a volcano
        beating a dark pulse
          beating a river of hot rock
        running beneath
        frozen stars
        to a distant prairie buried
          deep in cold wind.

THE WAY HOME

I feel like a star
        behind a cloud
        when wind blows me
                clear
now listen – words run together
        water over rocks
          washd smooth
        by ages
              elk shit
              bear shit
     coyote piss
          on sagebrush
     I was born
        in the wind
my nose cold from
          too many
winters and Mexico is the ghost
            of spring
    I want to see the high lakes
          of summer
      while the stars all laugh
            and blood paints
            a picture no voice
              can tell

20 jan 74
austin, texas

SO IT GOES

born in Havre to the tune
      of the Empire Builder
grew up in Chinook listening
        to mad chants
           of empty space
long sandbox hours spread
    from Cherry Ridge
          to the Bear Paws
drumming bison hoofs
        incantations of past lives
      fused with futures
           of strange flesh
lost in the prairies
      chasing prairie dogs
      across sagebrush
their tunnels hidden
        behind prickly pear forts
at an early age
        town was too small
          to get lost in
dreams of warm lust
      hay stacks of autumn dusk
hunting deer in Clear Creek brambles
    I struck out from all this
        to seek the world

                    of newspapers
            in strange cities tracing rumors
                        to far oceans
              swimming salt water strokes
              and meeting dark whores
                    in bleak latin streets
                   the refuse of centuries
        plying an ancient trade
                 we barterd flesh
                 in rented beds
                 sought pleasure
                 in the exchange
                        of genes
       we lost it all in a moment
                   of confusion
            the great silence suckt us
                up in a whiff
                    of sagebrush
              on a cold prairie night
        the Milky Way
                and the Northern Lights
            talking to each other
                    across the wind.

4 nov 75
missoula

WHAT THE BICENTENNIAL MEANS TO ME

    two hundred years
        human time
          trickles
            from a summer glacier
            flash frozen
                by a changing wind
        whole civilizations
            carved in mastodon ribs
        still covered with flesh
            wait some shift
            in nuclear orbit
        a universe pierced
            by a new rhythm
            of breathing

    two hundred years magnified
                like a supersonic jet
    cutting across blue sky
            popping a hard laugh
    at snow peaks glistening thru cloudscapes
                    far below
    a yowling of machines
            demanding
            their own architecture
    huge electrical circuits designing

    vast windows
     for a new brain
striving to think without blood
      creating sub-continents
      of human hamburger
quickly fried by micro-wave
     a tv-dinner
     consumed by cancer
     victims
who consult their credit cards
     before watching
     a sunset

two hundred years imposed like a tattoo
      on a grizzly's eyeball
an old indian stumbles crackt sidewalks
     following visions
     drownd in muscatel
surfaces in front of a used car lot
     finds himself
     violated
     for overtime parking
"FUCK YOU RIP!" he snarls
     and stumbles
     off like a tattoo
     artist run out
     of skin

    two hundred years gathered in a Great Circle
                dancing ghosts
                beat hot slash
                fire drums
howling clear cuts and smoke to scare
                tv sets
                into submission

what about all these red white and blue
                      fireworks and fist-pounding
                      speeches of progress?
hollow ringing of a liberty bell demise
                of the silver dollar
                    turning the corner
                            in a Japanese import
squeezing gasoline out of mescal
                          and throwing away
                          the vision filter
        – too clogged up –

a still breeze reflects sunlight
                  from shiny leaves
        a rubber tire
                sits in oily dust

    driven round and round two hundred years
                    carried
                   on its back
        deep in sub-atomic winds
             waiting out the storm
              and maybe a retread.

5 july 76
missoula

MILK RIVER BIRTHDAY
for my mother

    frozen streams curve
        thru stark brush
cold blue sky sprouts
        a cloud or two
the sun is almost warm
        a clatter of birds
        two dogs I can't
help but run groves
        of cottonwoods
    stand bare
along the river – nothing
        rides the air
old men melt in my blood
        I pump a fresh
          feeling to my lungs
a wildness clears my heart
        a voice speaks
        in the frozen river
    the trees wait.

1 apr 75
chinook

born April fool 1947 Havre Montana grew up 20 miles East in Chinook childhood prairie full of blizzards dusty summers Milk River floods usual adolescent frustrations manifested uniquely for my eventual edification playground battles lust fires burning at an early age altar boy sex fantasies at High Mass high school football failures day dreamed into war hero visions early mountain longings Bear Paws shimmering mid-summer blue from hot town sidewalks became college days in mountain enveloped Missoula ROTC scholarship subvertd by 1967 summer of love in Seattle pre-school artistic longings reawakened by hanging out with other confused wastrels of the times smoking weed tracing out lines of "what is real anyhow?" on canvases in notebooks on street corners first construction job that summer knocking down walls ON THE ROAD visions driving me beyond war hero fantasies to more immediate possibilities of life rather than glorious stupid death decided I'd rather get high with my friends than kill "gooks" first startd formalwriting Seattle summer 1968 trying to get work living on 1st avenue with B. McClure learning about time and life with no money a shift on the docks buys me a train ticket returnd to U of Mont for one last year met Roger Dunsmore who with many others helpd me beyond measure June 1969 hoppt a freight with a few friends for San Fran and began

my life as a wanderer served my Haight-Ashbury
time LSD education learnd to cook and wash
dishes like a regular macrobiotic champ drank
mucho beer and argued with J.W. 'till neither one
of us could see returnd to Montana the next
spring via hair raising ride with one Bowland
constantly scribbling thrown by inexorable
necessity into work situations became railroad
gandy dancer traveld winters in Mexico Central
and South America tired of that routine laid low
for a year now employd as construction worker
once more writing redneck work laments full of
concrete noise and jackhammer dust —

6 march 1977
missoula

DAVID E. THOMAS

DAVID E. THOMAS grew up on the Hi-Line in North-central Montana. He graduated from the University of Montana then found himself on the streets of San Francisco where he began his literary education. Economic realities drove him to work on railroad gangs, big construction projects like Libby Dam and other labor intensive jobs. He has traveled in the United States, Mexico and Central America. He has published four books of poems, *Fossil Fuel, Buck's Last Wreck, The Hellgate Wind* and *Waterworks Hill*. He has poems in the anthologies *The Last Best Place* and *Poems across the Big Sky* and *New Poets of the American West* and has recently published poems in Romania, *Blue Collar Review* and *Cedilla 6, 7* and *8*. Most recently his essay "Gothic Days" appeared in *The Complete Montana Gothic* edited by Peter Koch which also features Thomas's earliest published work. He currently lives in Missoula, Montana.

www.ingramcontent.com/pod-product-compliance
Lightning Source LLC
Chambersburg PA
CBHW031506040426
42444CB00007B/1224